NT TASTE LIKE C

te

ad UGH.

PING

What is it?

I'D RATHER
BE
IN TRAFFIC

G.R.O.S.S.

Miserable!

MEDIUM
FIRM... HUH?

NO
THANK
YOU!

Tee
Fool!

R PUDGY

TOFU
ME
ONCE!

SQUISHY

DOE

wh

bre

ZERO!

Soft

BO

HELLO?

TASTE?

are you there

FLAVOR?

anything

BLAND

SOY

BEANS...

NOTTA!

LOSE

THE

I Hate Tofu

COOKBOOK

35 RECIPES TO CHANGE YOUR MIND

TUCKER SHAW

ILLUSTRATIONS by JOEL HOLLAND

Stewart, Tabori & Chang, New York

CONTENTS

Tofu Chili
Tofu Salad (Kinda Like Egg Salad)
Curried Tofu Salad
Bibb Lettuce Salad with Tofu Green Goddess Dressing
Iceberg Wedge with Tofu Ranch Dressing
Tofu Caesar Salad

Main dishes, starring tofu.

Tofu Sloppy Joes
Tofu Noodle Toss
Smothered Tofuchiladas
Mac and Cheese
Tofu Parm
Tofu Balls
Garlic and Broccoli Tofu Stir-Fry
Red Wine and Mustard Tofu Bake

Recipes for outdoor grilling.

Grilled Tofu Kebabs
Asian Grilled Tofu Salad
Grilled Tofujitas
Grilled Tofu with Chimichurri

Dessert time. (Don't panic.)

Banana-Maple Tofu Pie
Salted Caramel Tofu "Cheesecake"
Peanut Butter–Chocolate Tofu Pie
Choco-Coco Banana Shake
Chocolate Pudding Pops
Strawberry-Gingersnap To-Fool

INTRODUCTION

HELLO,

I'm TOFU

Tofu. Say it out loud. "Tofu." Let the word just slide off your tongue. Notice how it rhymes with "Can't do"? With "old shoe"? With "Ew. EW!"?

I feel your horror. I used to hate tofu just as much as you do. More, maybe.

And it's hard to argue with tofu hatred, at least at first glance. There are few foods that turn people off as much as tofu, and not even just for the most obvious reasons: that it's an ugly shade of dirty eggshell; that it has a skeevy, spongy texture; and that it doesn't actually even look anything like food.

No, the real reason most people get turned off by tofu isn't because it's gross. It's because it seems SO BORING. But if tofu is considered boring rather than hateful, that represents progress. (That is, if you consider wider acceptance of tofu "progress," which is, I admit, a leap for tofu haters.)

See, when tofu was introduced to the United States in the middle of the last century, it was generally in gloppy, goopy, slimy, rubbery, tasteless dishes that tried desperately and unsuccessfully to stand in for proper things like meat. It was poorly treated by misguided, protein-starved people who probably didn't like food that much in the first place and therefore didn't care whether the final product tasted good or not.*

*This, of course, is a vast overstatement, but it's convenient for the purposes of this portion of the book so just go with it, if you will.

Flavor, schmavor

Here's where I blow your mind: The best thing tofu has to offer, and the thing that sets it apart from all other foods (well, most other foods), is its insistent boringness. This is a good thing.

Stay with me.

See, tofu really is tasteless. (Actually, it's more like flavorless, because tasteless means something else.) Good tofu tastes like . . . nothing, really. Nothing at all. But that lack of flavor, as it turns out, is tofu's greatest asset.

To use an analogy that I have a feeling you'll warm to: Tofu's flavorlessness is a lot like vodka's flavorlessness. You can do anything to it, add just about any flavoring or ingredient you like—sweet, salty, bitter, savory, sour, you name it—and it will support that flavor like a champ. Vodka, er, I mean tofu (sorry, distracted) will stay in the background, providing a solid base of protein for whatever else you feel like adding to it.

So what's the point of tofu, then, if it doesn't taste like anything? The point of tofu is that it's a clean, healthful, powerful, plant-based protein that provides all kinds of nutrients, not a lot of calories or carbohydrates, and pretty much no cholesterol. In oth-er words, it's food, and it's pretty good for you. (See page 14 for more on that front.)

No whammies

Here's something important to understand: This is not a vegetarian or vegan-focused cookbook. It's not a nondairy cookbook. You'll find milk, honey, cheese, mayo, and more nonvegan stuff like that in here. Maybe even the occasional crumble of bacon. But wherever I can, I'll point out possible substitutions if you want to eat vegan, and, besides, if you're a committed vegan, you probably have a bunch of workarounds already. But the point of this book isn't to avoid meat, it's just to add another option into your repertoire—a high-protein, low-fat, low-carb, low-cholesterol, gluten-free, calcium-rich, inexpensive, readily available option that also happens to be really easy to work with.

I'm not going to hit you with any wildly unusual ingredients. No agar-agar or hemp seeds or virgin coconut oil from the southern-facing slopes of Mount Matavanu here. Not that there's anything wrong with those things. They have their merits, but many of them are hard to find and not so cheap. Besides, since I'm an omnivore, I'm just as happy to use butter or chocolate.

I'm not trying to fool anyone into eating tofu. I hate recipes that try to fake people out. I'm not going to call it chicken if it isn't or a milkshake if it isn't. Although, if it's easier to explain what a particular dish is sort of like, I might do that. Like the Tofu Salad recipe on page 43. It's not egg salad, but you can kind of use it as such, so I've mentioned the words "egg salad" to give you a clue about what to expect (even though there aren't any eggs in it). There's one exception, which is Salted Caramel Tofu "Cheesecake" (page 85)—there's no other word for cheesecake.

In short, I don't think tofu should really be considered a substitute for meat or anything else. Tofu should stand alone as a legitimate food that's easy to cook with and, once you get the swing of it and get away from the goop and glop, ridiculously easy to like. You just have to give it a chance.

WHAT iS TOFU, ANYWAY?

Someone with experience in PR made a decision early on to go ahead and introduce tofu to the American market as *tofu* rather than what it really is: soybean curd. Not much of a ring to it, you know? "Get your gourmet soybean curd here!" Just can't really see that flying off the shelves.

So, marketers used a shorter version of the Japanese name (*tou fu*) which, at the time, had the benefit of not meaning much to most American supermarket goers. It was a clean slate. But mystery breeds distrust and people were slow to warm up to tofu because they just didn't know what it was or what to do with it. A plain, pale block of spongy white stuff stored in water? Suspicious at best.

But tofu isn't any weirder than, say, yogurt or cheese, really. It doesn't exactly grow on trees, but it doesn't fall all that far from the soybean plant.

How they make it

First, dried soybeans are soaked in water and processed into a paste. That paste is mixed with water into a slurry and cooked (often under pressure), then strained to remove the solids (which often go to the pig trough; hogs love the stuff). The remaining liquid is coagulated by mixing it with a coagulant like calcium sulfate or magnesium chloride (extracted from briny water like the Great Salt Lake in the same way we get sea salt from the ocean). This turns the soybean liquid back into a semisolid, kind of like cottage cheese (curds and whey, if you will).

Then, depending on what the final product is supposed to look and feel like (silken, firm, or extra-firm are the three basic types), the tofu is drained and pressed in a wooden (often bamboo) or metal pressing contraption. They put the screws on it, so to speak, to compress it and help it expel water. It's then pasteurized at 180°F (82°C) to make it a bit safer and more shelf-stable (much like milk), and, bingo, tofu ready for sale.

See? No weirder than yogurt, which was invented when Mongols stored milk in a sheep's stomach, tied it to a horse, and while galloping across the steppe, jostled and jiggled it around with a bunch of bacteria for long enough to ferment into something that keeps Jamie Lee Curtis regular.[*]

People have been making tofu for, like, thousands of years. No kidding: There's evidence that folks were eating it in China during the Han Dynasty in the second century B.C.E. So get on the bus already.

*Just saying.

SHOPPING & STORAGE

Buying tofu

Choose a style of tofu based on what you're going to use it for. There are three basic types, though you're likely to find even more variations depending on where you shop. Most tofu comes prepackaged in little square tubs containing about 14 ounces of tofu (sometimes 16 ounces). Not all grocery stores are consistent about where they keep it, but the produce area is the first place I always look, and it's there probably 60 percent of the time. Occasionally you'll find tofu near the cheese or dairy. So, good luck.

Silken tofu

Silken tofu is soft and yogurtlike. Smushy. Silky (get it?). It hasn't had much liquid extracted, and it hasn't been formed into blocks. This is the best tofu for things like smoothies or dips, or for other things that are supposed to be soft, like pudding or custard pies.

Firm tofu

Firm tofu is the most popular kind. It comes in a solid but pliable block with a fairly high water content. It's easy to crumble and to slice. For most recipes, before you use it, you should press or squeeze it to get the water out (see page 11).

Extra-firm tofu

It doesn't take a genius to figure this one out. It's firmer than firm tofu, has less moisture in it, and is easier to cut into distinct cubes. Extra-firm is aces for things like pan-frying or grilling because it holds its shape and doesn't fall apart very easily, even after a squeeze.

Other types of tofu

You might also find "lite" tofu, both firm and silken, which has a bit less fat and/or calories (and not quite as smooth a texture), and flavored tofu. Skip the flavored tofu because, at best, it will taste overflavored and, at worst, it will taste totally artificial. Besides, you're going to add your own flavor to the tofu, and you want to control it yourself.

And forget tofu that's already cut into blocks. It typically costs twice as much, and it takes pretty much no time at all to cut up your own tofu (see page 12).

If you chose the right neighborhood to live in, you have an Asian market or restaurant nearby that makes and sells fresh tofu. If you've never had a dish of warm, fresh tofu, you're in for a nearly indescribable treat, which I will here attempt to describe: Imagine a bowl full of soft, cozy, savory, silky, milky, creamy pudding. (OK, I failed, but try it if you can.) Lovely with a chilly glass of bubbly.

Storing tofu

Just like meat and milk and ex-lovers, tofu can get a little funky if it hangs around
too long. Avoid that. For starters, always check the sell-by date before you make
a purchase.

Firm and extra-firm tofu is sold packed in water. When you open the package,
slice what you need off the block, drop what is left in an airtight plastic container,
cover it with fresh water, and keep it in the refrigerator. It should last 3 to 5 days. But
do yourself (and your tofu) a favor and change the water every day, especially if the
water starts to look cloudy or muddy.

If you're not sure if the tofu is still fresh, give it a whiff. Fresh tofu doesn't smell
like anything at all, but old or "off" tofu has a mild, sour reek. If you have suspicions,
or smell old socks rather than fresh water, toss it. It's sad to throw away unused food,
but it's no good any more, so let it go. Console yourself with a new block or two of tofu.
After all, it's relatively inexpensive, and well, better safe than stomach achey.

You also can freeze tofu for about three months. Just make sure you press it first.
Freezing is more than a storage fix, it's also a useful cooking technique that can lead
to more intensely-flavored tofu (see page 13).

If you have lots of leftover tofu that's close to its expiration date and you just
can't bring yourself to ditch it, crumble it, fry it up in a nonstick skillet, and stick it in
the fridge. Cooked, it should last a few extra days. Just toss it into a stir-fry or soup,
and you'll be good.

PREPPiNG TOFU

Tofu is the easiest thing in the world to cook with. OK, that's an overstatement, but only just barely. You do need to do a bit of prep on it before you start to cook, but it's certainly no more complicated than preparing vegetables and meat or anything else. It takes almost no effort, but it will take a little bit of time.

A pressing issue

Before you use firm or extra-firm tofu, you'd best press it. (If you're using silken tofu, you're off the hook, and you can sit this part out.) Pressing tofu helps remove excess water to make it easier to control while it's cooking, and to make room for everything else you're going to add to it.

The best way to press tofu is with a tofu press. I know, I know. More equipment! Look, I'm an avowed antigadget fanatic. I hate having more tools in the kitchen. But I actually broke down and bought a tofu press, and I'm glad I did. It makes pressing tofu easier and keeps the kitchen cleaner. You can buy a cheap one for under $20 or a ritzy one for north of $100 (bonus: the pricey one will likely be nice enough to keep on your kitchen counter, sparking all sorts of spirited conversation). Cheap or expensive, most tofu presses on the market should get the job done nicely if you follow the ridiculously simple (usually pictograph-style) directions that come with it.

If you don't have a tofu press and aren't yet committed enough to the whole idea of tofu to buy one, I fully support MacGyvering the situation and pressing your tofu DIY style. Here's how:

1. First, plan ahead about an hour or so (OK, maybe 30 minutes will cut it). It takes a bit of time to get the water out.
2. Line a rimmed baking sheet or a big plate with a dishtowel, then three or four layers of paper towels.
3. Slice the block of tofu into five or six smaller blocks and lay them on top of the dishtowel. Then drape a few paper towels over the top of the tofu.
4. Place another baking sheet or plate on top of the paper towels, then weigh it down evenly with something heavy, like a few cans of beans, a bag of dried beans, or a heavy pot, or a baby goat or something.*
5. If you have room in the fridge, slip the whole shebang in there. But if you're only going to press it for 30 minutes or an hour, you can leave it out on the counter.

And there you have it. After 30 minutes or so, you'll start to notice that the paper towels and dishtowel are damp and the tofu is lighter and dryer. Keep going for another 30 minutes; you'll be surprised at how much moisture comes out. If you're willing to go overnight in the fridge, you'll have tofu that's positively thirsty for whatever flavors you want to feed it. And that's right where you want it to be.

Of course, if you're hungry and want to get cooking, you can get away with most of the recipes in this book without pressing it much at all, like smoothies for example. So don't sweat it too much if you just can't wait.

*Actually, don't use a baby goat, they never stay still.

Cutting tofu

For large tofu slabs, cut a tofu block in half through the middle like you're splitting a mattress into two less-thick mattresses. For smaller slabs, cut the slim mattresses in half lengthwise. For sticks, cut the slim mattresses into sticks 1 inch (2.5 cm) wide. For cubes, cut the 1-inch (2.5-cm) sticks width-wise into cubes.

A FEW TOFU TRICKS

Just as with family members and significant others, a little manipulation goes a long way. Sometimes, giving your tofu a little extra nudge will help you to get the most out of it.

Freeze it

Try freezing tofu for at least 24 hours after you press it. The leftover water in the tofu expands when it freezes, creating little pockets in the tofu. As it thaws back to room temperature, much of this water seeps out rather than absorbing back into the tofu (press it again to really get the full effect); the vacating water makes room for marinades and flavorings. Come to think of it, if you freeze the tofu, you probably want to use a little less marinade or a marinade that's not as intensely seasoned (use less salt!); otherwise, you'll overdo it, and your final dish will taste too strong.

Marinate It

Tofu absorbs marinade—truly absorbs it—better than almost anything else. Way better than meat, for example. So, marinate away, but be careful. Don't overdo it. Use plenty of marinade, but don't go bonkers or you'll have too much flavor (especially salt) and your face will pucker up like a Ricky Gervais bathtub selfie. You might even end up calling in a pizza, which was what you were trying to avoid in the first place.

Use marinades without much oil. Oil doesn't really work well with tofu, because of all the water in it (even after you press it, it has a high water content). And you know, oil and water, they just don't jibe—so if you have an oily marinade, you'll just end up with a layer of grease on the tofu. Not cute.

Make it crisp

If you plan to fry or bake the tofu and want it to come out crisp, cornstarch is your friend. It adheres nicely to tofu and cooks up to a delicate, light crunch. Shake cubes of tofu and a couple tablespoons of cornstarch in a plastic bag, or dredge it like you would to fry chicken or pork cutlets.

BORiNG BUT IMPORTANT *

Tofu is a great source of protein without a lot of baggage. One serving contains 10 grams of protein and just about 100 calories. You'll find 5 grams of fat in there and no cholesterol. That's a much better protein-to-calorie ratio than you'll find in beef or cheese, which are both heavy with cholesterol and fat.

Asleep yet? Tofu also has a decent amount of calcium, iron, and other nutrients, especially minerals like manganese and selenium. It's not really a vitamin power-house and has no fiber to speak of, but its glycemic index is very low (it doesn't spike your blood sugar), and, did I mention how much protein it packs?

*The "important" part of this chapter is debatable.
It's only important if you care about this kind of stuff.

According to the FDA, here are the nutritional numbers for a half-cup (4-ounce/115-g) serving of firm tofu.

NUTRIENT	AMOUNT	PERCENT OF DAILY VALUE
Vitamin A	0 IU	0%
Vitamin C	0.3 mg	0%
Vitamin K	3 mcg	4%
Vitamin B6	0.1 mg	4%
Calcium	253 mg	25%
Iron	2 mg	1%
Magnesium	46.6 mg	12%
Potassium	186 mg	5%
Copper	0.3 mg	14%
Manganese	0.8 mg	39%
Cholesterol	0 mg	0%
Fat (Saturated Fat)	5.3 g (1.1 g)	8% (5%)
Fiber	1.1 g	5%
Protein	10.3 g	21%
Carbohydrates	2.1 g	1%

CH. 1

MORNING, SUNSHINE!

QUICK BREAKFASTS TO GET YOU GOING.

Here's one huge advantage tofu has over other foods: It's way faster and easier to deal with than, say, French toast or oatmeal. And, in the morning, when your eyes are bleary and your stomach is impatient, that's no small thing. Pro tip: Do your pressing the night before so your tofu's all ready to go when you rise and shine.

Who says the only thing you can scramble is an egg? Not me. This is a savory, healthy, satisfying breakfast that will either send you running around the block in a fit of physical virtuousness, or send you back to bed for a happy, restorative post-breakfast nap, which is the best thing in the world. Add whatever you want to this scramble: shredded carrot, brussels sprouts, some black beans, you name it. Serve with buttered toast or an English muffin, or diner style with ketchup, or wrapped up in warm tortillas drizzled with hot sauce. Serves 4.

INGREDIENTS

1 tablespoon butter or olive oil

1 medium yellow onion, finely chopped

2 cups (310 g) frozen hash browns, defrosted

½ teaspoon salt

1 cup (180 g) finely chopped cooked broccoli (frozen is OK, but defrost it and drain thoroughly)

1 package (14 ounces/400 g) firm tofu, drained, pressed, and crumbled

1 cup (100 g) shredded cheese or nondairy cheese substitute

3 scallions, chopped

1 Heat the butter or oil in a large, heavy skillet until foaming (if using butter) or shimmering (if using oil).

2 Add the onion, hash browns, and salt and cook until the onion is golden, about 10 minutes. Add the broccoli and cook for 3 minutes more. Add the tofu and cook for 2 minutes, stirring frequently.

3 Remove the pan from the heat and stir in the cheese. Sprinkle with the scallions.

TOFU
SCRAMBLE

Tropical Smoothie

Smoothies are just so great in the morning. I mean, you can get a meal in you without chewing. This makes one big, delicious, healthy smoothie that tastes like you're on a Tahitian vacation. Serves 1.

INGREDIENTS

½ cup (115 g) silken tofu
1 cup (240 ml) very cold vanilla-flavored coconut milk, plus more as needed
½ cup (85 g) frozen chopped pineapple
½ cup (85 g) frozen chopped mango
1 banana, sliced and frozen
¼ cup (20 g) rolled oats
1 cup (120 ml) crushed ice

Everything into the blender. Start it on low to incorporate the ingredients, then let it rip on liquefy until everything's fully blended. You might need to stop the blender and tap it once or twice to release air bubbles. If you need more liquid, add more coconut milk.

Maple-Berry Smoothie

Don't sweat the spinach here: You won't taste it, but it's good for you. Serves 1.

INGREDIENTS

½ cup (115 g) silken tofu
1 cup (240 ml) soy milk, almond milk, or regular milk, plus more as needed
1 cup (150 g) frozen mixed berries
1 banana, sliced and frozen
½ cup (60 g) frozen spinach
2 tablespoons maple syrup
1 cup (240 ml) crushed ice

Everything into the blender. Start it on low to incorporate the ingredients together, then liquefy until everything's fully blended. You might need to stop the blender and tap it once or twice to release air bubbles. If you need more liquid, add more milk.

Mochaccino Peanut Smoothie

This is a great preworkout smoothie, and a slick way to combine your coffee and breakfast into one serving. You'll have a caffeine buzz for the rest of the morning, or at least until you can make it to Starbucks. Serves 1.

INGREDIENTS

½ cup (115 g) silken tofu
1 cup (240 ml) coffee, cold
   (leftover from yesterday
   is fine), plus more as
   needed
2 tablespoons
   chocolate syrup
3 tablespoons
   creamy peanut
   butter
1 cup (240 ml)
   crushed ice

Everything into the blender. Start it on low to incorporate the ingredients, then let it rip on liquefy until everything's fully blended. You might need to stop the blender and tap it once or twice to release air bubbles. If you need more liquid, add more coffee.

CH. 2

MUNCHIES

SNACKS TO TIDE YOU OVER—
OR SOAK UP THE BOOZE.

It's midafternoon, and you could use a little . . . something. Or maybe it's cocktail hour, and what's a drink without a little nosh? Or it's game day and you're settled in front of the TV. Whatever, you're hungry. Grab a bag of potato chips if you like (I'm all for potato chips), or make one of these snacks and feel just a little better about yourself.

This is a good, chunky, healthy take on guacamole that might horrify guacamole purists but that the rest of us will like because it tastes good, and it has an extra bonus: protein. Just as for guacamole, serve this with tortilla chips. Makes about 2 cups (480 g).

INGREDIENTS
½ package (7 ounces/200 g) firm tofu, drained, pressed, and crumbled
2 ripe avocados, pitted, peeled, and cut into small pieces
1 cup (260 g) salsa
Juice of 1 or 2 limes
Pinch of coarse salt
Drizzle of hot sauce (optional)

Stir it all together in a medium bowl and taste. Add more lime juice or hot sauce, if desired. Let sit in the fridge, covered, for an hour, or up to 1 day. Bring it out about 30 minutes before serving—it's best at room temperature.

These are kind of like mozzarella sticks, so if you're up for it, serve these with a little bowlful of pizza sauce or marinara sauce for dipping. You can easily double the recipe. Serves 4.

INGREDIENTS

2 tablespoons cornstarch
1 teaspoon onion powder
1 teaspoon garlic powder or ground granulated garlic
½ teaspoon salt
1 tablespoon granulated sugar
1 or 2 large eggs
1 cup (100 g) panko bread crumbs
1 package (14 ounces/400 g) extra-firm tofu, drained, pressed, and cut into 12 sticks

1 Preheat the oven to 375°F (190°C) and line a baking sheet with parchment paper.

2 Line up three shallow bowls on the counter. In the first, stir together the cornstarch, onion powder, garlic powder or ground garlic, salt, and sugar. In the second, beat an egg. Put the bread crumbs in the third.

3 Working with one tofu stick at a time, coat it first with the cornstarch mixture. Knock off the excess and dunk it in the egg. Let the egg drip off and drop it in the bread crumbs, generously coating the tofu. Place it on the prepared baking sheet and continue with the remaining tofu. You may need another beaten egg.

4 Slide the pan into the oven and bake for about 45 minutes, turning once or twice. When the tofu is firm and crisp, it's ready. Eat it hot.

FRENCH ONION TOFU DIP

Oh, yes. This is where you get out that bag of Ruffles and go nuts. The key here is patience, however, because the onions take a long time to cook down to where you want them to be. And you also want to slip the dip into the fridge for an hour or so before you eat it so the flavors have a chance to meld together. You can make this with tofu sour cream if you can find it—just eliminate the vinegar and mustard. Makes about 3 cups (720 ml).

INGREDIENTS

3 large yellow onions, sliced thin

2 tablespoons butter

1 tablespoon granulated sugar

½ teaspoon salt

1 package (12 ounces/340 g) silken tofu

1 teaspoon garlic powder

1 tablespoon distilled white vinegar

2 tablespoons Dijon mustard

2 tablespoons minced fresh chives

Freshly ground black pepper

1 Put the onions and butter in a large skillet over medium heat. (It will look like a lot of onions, but they cook down quite a bit.) Sprinkle the sugar and salt over the top. Cook, stirring frequently, until the onions are a deep golden brown, about 20 minutes. Remove from the heat to let cool.

2 Vigorously stir together the tofu, garlic powder, vinegar, and mustard in a medium bowl until completely combined. Adjust the flavors to taste, if needed. Stir in the onions. Refrigerate for at least 1 hour or up to 24 hours, stirring once or twice while it chills.

3 Sprinkle the chives over the top, give it a few grinds of black pepper, and allow the dip to come to room temperature before serving with whatever chip you dig. Or spread it on a roast beef sandwich.

Tofu's greatest weakness—its flavorlessness—is its greatest strength in this case. Tofu just provides a framework for all the other sweet-and-spicy flavors going on here. Plan ahead, because this needs to marinate for one hour before you bake it. Serves 4.

INGREDIENTS

¼ cup (60 ml) maple syrup
3 tablespoons soy sauce
3 tablespoons barbecue
   sauce
2 tablespoons sriracha
2 teaspoons white wine
   vinegar
1 tablespoon cornstarch
2 packages (28 ounces/795 g)
   extra-firm tofu, drained,
   pressed, and cut into
   1-inch (2.5-cm) cubes

1 In a wide, shallow bowl, whisk together the syrup, soy sauce, barbecue sauce, sriracha, vinegar, and cornstarch until thoroughly incorporated. Add the tofu and stir to coat. Marinate at room temperature for 1 hour.

2 Preheat the oven to 375°F (190°C). Arrange the tofu in a single layer in a 9-by-13-inch (23-by-33-cm) baking dish and bake, stirring once or twice, for about 45 minutes. The nuggets are ready when they're firm to the touch. Eat 'em while they're hot.

SWEET & SPICY TOFU NUGGETS

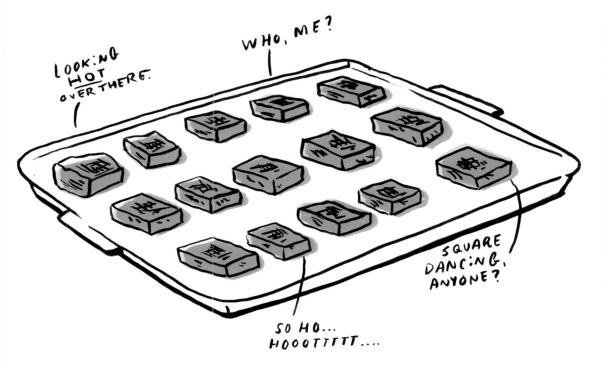

When you add tofu to hummus, something really great happens: It's softer. I know, you're thinking, "Big whoop." But think about it. How many times have you broken a pita chip in hummus that's too hard? How many times have you had to spoon it out and smash it onto your sandwich rather than being able to spread it? I'm just asking. You can buy tahini at the grocery store; it's a sesame paste that adds a little necessary something to hummus. I like my hummus lemony, so this recipe calls for all the juice from a lemon, but if you'd like to leave out some or all of that, go for it. It's your hummus, not mine. Ditto if you'd like more garlic flavor, or more heat, or . . . whatever. Make this at least an hour before you plan to serve it, so the flavors have a chance to meld and relax. Makes about 2 cups (480 g).

INGREDIENTS

1 can (14 ounces/400 g) chickpeas, drained
1 large garlic clove, smashed and minced
1 large piece of roasted red pepper, minced (about ¼ cup/60 g)
1 cup (225 g) silken tofu
2 tablespoons tahini
2 tablespoons plus 1 teaspoon olive oil
Juice of 1 lemon
½ teaspoon salt
½ teaspoon red pepper flakes (optional)
Fresh parsley leaves

1 Put the chickpeas, garlic, roasted red pepper, tofu, tahini, 2 tablespoons of the oil, lemon juice, and salt in a food processor and let it rip. Taste and adjust the flavor, if needed. Spoon into a medium bowl and slip it into the fridge for 1 hour.

2 Take the hummus out of the fridge about 15 minutes before serving. Give it a stir, then drizzle with the remaining tea-spoon oil and sprinkle with the red pepper flakes (if using) and parsley. Serve with pita chips or vegetables or spread it on a sandwich. Or you can just spoon it greedily into your mouth. Your call.

RED PEPPER TOFU HUMMUS

CH. 3

NOONERS

SOUPS & SALADS FOR
MIDDAY MEALS.

Tofu's a simple thing to add to soup or salad if you want to bump up the protein content without adding a lot of fat and calories. Even if you aren't on a diet or anything, that's a good thing, right? Right.

VEGGIE SOUP

"VERY DELICIOUS"
:N DUTCH

ERGILEKKER

MMMM
(((,))

(is universal)

When you are legitimately sick in bed, nothing beats chicken soup. But if you're even just a little bit ill, or tired of chicken soup, or you'd just rather eat something that's all vegetables and not meaty at all, or if you're not remotely sick but just want a nice bowl of fresh-tasting soup—here's your dish. Serves 4 to 6.

INGREDIENTS

2 tablespoons olive oil
1 medium onion, chopped
2 medium carrots, peeled and chopped
2 stalks celery, chopped
1 teaspoon salt
2 cloves garlic, smashed and minced
1 quart (960 ml) low-sodium vegetable stock
2 tablespoons soy sauce
1 bunch kale, stemmed and leaves cut into 1-inch (2.5-cm) pieces
1 can (14 ounces/400 g) white beans, rinsed and drained
1 package (14 ounces/400 g) firm tofu, drained, pressed, and cubed
1 cup (125 g) frozen peas, green beans, corn, edamame, or a mix
Salt and black pepper

1 Heat the oil in a Dutch oven over medium-high heat until it's shimmering. Add the onion, carrots, celery, and salt and cook until soft and starting to brown, about 10 minutes. Add the garlic and cook for 1 minute more. Add the stock and soy sauce and stir until it comes to a boil, scraping up any browned bits on the bottom of the pan. Lower the heat to a simmer for 10 minutes.

2 Add the kale, beans, tofu, and 2 cups (480 ml) water and return to a simmer. Simmer for 5 minutes, then add the frozen vegetables. Add more water if needed.

3 Add salt and pepper to taste and serve with a grilled cheese sandwich if it's raining out.

SPICY SPINACH, LEMON & TOFU SOUP

Sometimes soup should be soothing, but other times it should be invigorating, like this one. Serve this when your nose is clogged up, or whenever you want your soup to make you stand up and say "Ma'am, yes ma'am! May I have another?" Serves 4.

INGREDIENTS

2 tablespoons olive oil

1 teaspoon red pepper flakes

2 medium onions, chopped

1 medium carrot, peeled and diced

1 package (14 ounces/400 g) firm tofu, drained, pressed, and cubed

6 cups (1.4 L) vegetable stock

1 bag (about 5 ounces/ 140 g) baby spinach or 1 cup (120 g) frozen

Juice of 2 lemons

Salt and black pepper

1 Heat the oil in a Dutch oven over medium-high heat. Add the red pepper flakes and cook until fragrant, about 2 minutes. Add the onions and carrot and cook until soft, about 10 minutes. Add the tofu and cook, stirring frequently, until just starting to turn golden, 4 to 6 minutes. Add the stock and 2 cups (480 ml) water. Bring to a simmer and cook for 10 minutes.

2 Turn off the heat and stir in the spinach and lemon juice. Season with salt and pepper to taste. Serve with a big hunk of bread.

Tofu chili is a perfect way to use tofu because it just soaks up all the other flavors and, without being intrusive, adds a nice pop of texture. You can improvise all you want with this recipe: different vegetables, different beans, and different seasonings and spices. Your call. Just like a meat-based chili, this actually tastes better on the day after it's made, when you can reheat it and eat it in front of an old movie. It's also good at room temperature, so take it to the office and save yourself the eleven bucks you'd otherwise pay for a tossed salad. Serves 4 to 6.

INGREDIENTS

2 tablespoons olive oil
2 medium yellow onions, chopped
1 medium red onion, chopped
1 large green bell pepper, seeded and chopped
2 tablespoons chili powder
1 teaspoon ground cumin (optional)
2 large garlic cloves, smashed and chopped
1 chile packed in adobo, chopped
2 cans (29 ounces/822 g) diced tomatoes (with juice)
1 can (14 ounces/400 g) pinto beans, rinsed and drained
2 cups (480 ml) chicken or vegetable stock
1 package (14 ounces/400 g) extra-firm tofu, drained, pressed, and crumbled
1 cup (40 g) packed fresh cilantro leaves, chopped

1   Heat the oil in a Dutch oven over medium-high heat. Add the onions and bell pepper and cook until soft and golden, about 10 minutes. Add the chili powder and cumin, if using, and cook until fragrant, about 2 minutes. Add the garlic and chopped chile and cook for 2 minutes. Add the tomatoes (with juice) and cook for 2 minutes. Add the beans and stock and bring to a simmer. Stir in the tofu and continue to simmer, uncovered, for about 30 minutes.

2   Serve with the cilantro.

TOFU SALAD
(KINDA LIKE EGG SALAD)

I promised up front that I wasn't going to play that game that so many people play, calling something eggs or meat when that's not what it is. But there's really no other way to describe this salad, which acts and eats like egg salad even though it's not. Some tofu "egg" salad recipes call for a teaspoon or so of turmeric, which is an intensely yellow spice that, if you do have it in your cupboard, will give this a nice color, but if you don't have it, you can easily skip it because it doesn't add that much flavor anyway. This works great in sandwiches, but if you're not eating bread, use it in lettuce wraps. Serves 4.

INGREDIENTS
1 package (14 ounces/400 g) firm tofu, drained, pressed, and crumbled
½ cup (120 ml) mayonnaise or Vegenaise
3 tablespoons Dijon mustard
1 stalk celery, chopped
1 tablespoon white wine vinegar
3 scallions, chopped
3 tablespoons capers, drained (optional)
Pinch each of salt and black pepper

Stir everything together in a medium bowl, then let it sit for 15 minutes. Adjust the seasonings, as necessary, and eat. You can keep this in the fridge for 2 to 3 days.

CURRIED TOFU SALAD

This reminds me of that standard curried chicken salad you see everywhere, from department store cafés to big-box discount grocery retailers. Except without the chicken, so there's that. Anyway, it's the curry that really matters here. Add as much or as little as you like. Eat either on bread as a sandwich or scooped onto a plate with lettuce. Serves 4.

INGREDIENTS

1 package (14 ounces/400 g) firm tofu, drained, pressed, and crumbled

½ cup (120 ml) mayonnaise or Vegenaise

1 to 2 tablespoons curry powder

1 carrot, peeled and shredded

1 celery stick, diced

½ cup (80 g) golden raisins

½ cup (50 g) sliced almonds

Pinch each of salt and black pepper

Stir everything together in a medium bowl and serve. Store in an airtight container in the refrigerator for up to 3 days.

Just when you thought Green Goddess dressing couldn't get any more hippie-dippy . . . I added tofu to it! I know, try to contain your enthusiasm. But tofu really works great here, giving the dressing a nice silky feel (that's "mouthfeel" to you foodies). By the way, I know tofu is vegan and all, but a few crumbled bacon bits on this salad is really great. Just saying. Croutons are good, too. Serves 4.

INGREDIENTS

1 cup (225 g) silken tofu
1 cup (40 g) fresh basil
    leaves, chopped
½ cup (45 g) chopped fresh
    parsley leaves
1 large garlic clove,
    smashed
Pinch each of salt and black
    pepper
Juice of 1 lime
¼ cup (60 ml) olive oil
2 heads Bibb lettuce, leaves
    rinsed and dried
5 scallions, chopped
1 avocado, pitted, peeled,
    and diced

1 Put the tofu, basil, parsley, garlic, salt and pepper, and lime juice in a blender and blend on medium speed until incorporated. With the blender running on low, slowly pour in the oil until it all emulsifies.

2 Place a few lettuce leaves each on four plates, then sprinkle with the scallions and avocado. Douse with dressing. Yum.

BiBB LETTUCE SALAD w/ TOFU GREEN GODDESS DRESSING

ICEBERG WEDGE w/ TOFU RANCH DRESSING

What's wrong with ranch dressing? Nothing. Nothing at all. The tofu really adds a nice silky texture to this dressing, so it works spooned over an iceberg wedge or as a dip for vegetables or potato chips. This makes enough dressing that you might have some left over, even after making four salads. Lucky you. Serves 4.

INGREDIENTS

½ cup (120 ml) olive oil
1 cup (225 g) silken tofu
¼ cup (60 ml) mayonnaise
   or Vegenaise
¼ cup (60 ml) sour cream
½ teaspoon salt
½ teaspoon black pepper
1 tablespoon distilled white
   vinegar
1 teaspoon onion powder
1 teaspoon garlic powder or
   ground granulated garlic
½ teaspoon dried dill
¼ cup (10 g) fresh parsley
   leaves, coarsely chopped
Juice of 1 lemon
1 teaspoon paprika
1 large head iceberg lettuce,
   chilled

1 Put all the ingredients except the lettuce into the blender and let it rip for about 2 minutes, or until thoroughly incorporated and emulsified. If the dressing is too stiff, whisk in a tablespoon or so of water.

2 Remove the outer leaves from the lettuce and cut it into four wedges. Spoon the dressing over the top and serve.

Was the Caesar salad invented in Los Angeles or Tijuana? Who knows? Not me. I'm happy just eating it. The tofu in this recipe adds some protein (which is good), but it also adds clinginess, which is what you want in a rich dressing like this. The anchovies are optional, but you'll be missing out if you don't use them. Serve with very cold martinis. Serves 4.

INGREDIENTS
¼ cup (60 ml) olive oil, plus more as needed
1 large garlic clove, smashed
2 anchovy fillets, plus more for serving (optional)
1 tablespoon red wine vinegar
2 tablespoons Dijon mustard
1 teaspoon soy sauce
1 cup (225 g) silken tofu
Juice of 1 lemon, plus more as needed
¼ cup (25 g) shredded Parmesan cheese, plus more for serving
Salt and black pepper
3 hearts of Romaine lettuce, chopped
Croutons, for serving

1 Put the oil, garlic, anchovies (if using), vinegar, mustard, soy sauce, tofu, and lemon juice in a blender and blend on medium speed until completely incorporated, about 2 minutes. Add the Parmesan and blend for 1 more minute. Try the dressing and add the salt and pepper to taste and more lemon juice, if needed. (If it's too stiff, add more oil, a tablespoon at a time, until you get the right consistency.)

2 In a large bowl, drizzle the dressing over the lettuce, toss, and serve garnished with additional anchovies (if using), Parmesan, and croutons.

TOFU CAESAR SALAD

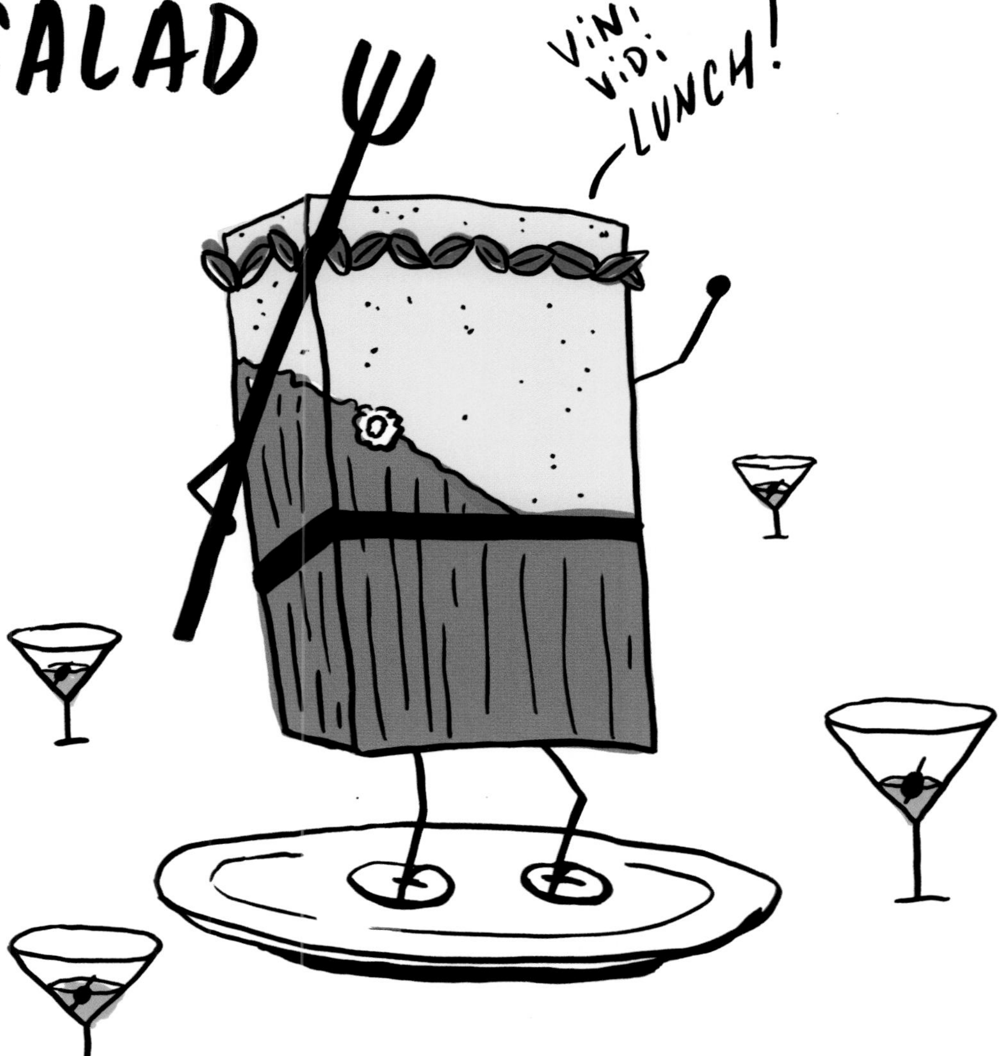

CH. 4

MARQUEE ACTS

MAIN DISHES, STARRING TOFU.

You could always go the Tofurky route, or whatever other fake-meat route you want, but I'm not on board. I hate the inauthenticity of calling things something that they aren't, and I don't care what you do to it, tofu isn't meat. That said, there are some flavor cues we can take from meaty dishes like chicken Parmesan or beef enchiladas and apply them to tofu. Why not? It sucks up flavor like a thirsty sponge.

You'd think that the secret to a great sloppy joe is the meat and spices. You'd be close, but no cigar: The real secret is delicious buttered, griddled rolls. This recipe makes gooey, messy sloppy joes. Serve them with French fries. Serves 4.

INGREDIENTS

1 tablespoon olive oil

1 medium onion, diced

1 medium green bell pepper, seeded and diced

2 tablespoons soy sauce

¼ teaspoon cayenne pepper

1 package (14 ounces/400 g) firm tofu, drained, pressed, and crumbled

1 can (14½ ounces/411 g) diced tomatoes, drained

1 can (14 ounces/400 g) pinto beans, rinsed and drained

2 tablespoons ketchup

1 tablespoon Dijon mustard

2 tablespoons butter, softened

4 hamburger buns

1 Heat the oil in a Dutch oven over medium-high heat. Add the onion and bell pepper and cook until the onion is soft and starting to brown, 12 to 14 minutes. Stir in the soy sauce and cayenne pepper. Add the tofu and cook until the tofu soaks up the sauce.

2 Add the tomatoes, beans, ketchup, and mustard and stir until combined. Reduce the heat to low and simmer for about 10 minutes.

3 Butter the inside surfaces of each bun. Heat up a large skillet or griddle to high and cook the buns, buttered-side down, until they are browned and hot, about 3 minutes. Spoon the sloppy joe mixture into the buns and serve.

TOFU NOODLE TOSS

This recipe makes the most of what little dried ramen noodles have to offer. This should make enough for everyone, but you might find you eat it all yourself, in which case have a number for takeout handy to appease your guests. Serves 4.

INGREDIENTS

2 tablespoons soy sauce
2 tablespoons rice wine vinegar
1 package (14 ounces/400 g) extra-firm tofu, drained, pressed, and cubed
2 teaspoons vegetable oil
1 medium onion, sliced
1 cup (70 g) sliced button or shiitake mushrooms
2 cups (140 g) coleslaw mix
2 packages (6 ounces/170 g) dried ramen noodles (flavor packets discarded), cooked and drained
1 tablespoon sesame oil
1 handful bean sprouts
Lime wedges, for serving

1 In a medium bowl, stir together the soy sauce and vinegar. Add the tofu and stir to coat. Let sit at room temperature for 30 minutes.

2 Meanwhile, in a large, deep skillet, add the vegetable oil and onion and cook over medium-high heat until the onion is soft but not yet browned, about 6 minutes. Add the mushrooms and cook for 3 minutes. Add the tofu to the skillet (reserving the marinade). Cook for 8 minutes, or until the tofu starts to brown. Add the coleslaw mix and cook until heated through.

3 Reduce the heat to medium. Add the noodles and toss. Pour over the reserved marinade and toss. Drizzle the sesame oil over all.

4 Divide the noodles among four bowls, top with the bean sprouts, and serve with lime wedges.

What's not to love about a big baking dish full of rolled and smothered enchiladas? This is a delicious all-in-one meal that everyone at the table will dive into greedily when you bring it out all bubbling and hot. Even if you're by yourself, you'll be knocking imaginary elbows out of the way. The extra adobo sauce is optional and is only recommended if you like your enchiladas pretty hot; you can skip it or add more or less to taste. This is great for breakfast the next day. Serves 6.

INGREDIENTS

2 tablespoons olive oil

2 medium onions, chopped

1 tablespoon chili powder

2 garlic cloves, smashed
    and minced

1 chipotle chile in adobo,
    chopped

1 tablespoon adobo sauce
    from the chile (optional)

2 packages (28 ounces/
    795 g) firm tofu, drained,
    pressed, and crumbled

1 can (14 ounces/400 g)
    black beans, drained

2 cups (200 g) shredded
    Cheddar and/or Jack
    cheese

2 cups (490 g) enchilada
    sauce

12 (6-inch/15-cm) corn
    tortillas

1 Preheat the oven to 375°F (190°C). In a large, deep skillet, heat the oil over medium-high heat. Add the onions and cook until soft but not yet brown, about 6 minutes. Add the chili powder and cook until fragrant, just 30 seconds. Add the garlic and stir. Add the chipotle chile and adobo sauce, if using, and stir. Cook for 2 minutes, then add the tofu and stir to coat. Add the beans, 1 cup of the cheese, and 1 cup of the enchilada sauce.

2 Working with one tortilla at a time, wrap the tofu mixture into the tortilla and nestle into a 9-by-13-inch (23-by-33-cm) baking dish. When all the tortillas are rolled and placed in the pan, douse everything with the remaining cup enchilada sauce and sprinkle with the remaining cup cheese.

3 Cover the dish tightly with foil and bake for 20 minutes, then remove the foil and bake for 10 minutes more. Serve with lots of beer.

SMOTHERED TOFUCHILADAS

Unlike so-called "real" macaroni and cheese, this cheater's version uses two kinds of tofu to make the cheesy part all silky and smooth without a béchamel base. That means you can get away with making mac and cheese without having to cook flour and milk first. Serves 4 to 6.

INGREDIENTS

2 tablespoons butter, melted, plus more for the pan

¼ package (3½ ounces/ 100 g) firm tofu, drained, pressed, and cubed

1 cup (225 g) silken tofu

1 teaspoon Worcestershire sauce

1 teaspoon garlic powder or ground granulated garlic

1 teaspoon onion powder

½ teaspoon salt

1 teaspoon black pepper

½ cup (120 ml) chicken or vegetable stock, plus more as needed

2 cups (200 g) shredded cheese (Cheddar, Jack, mozzarella, Fontina, or better yet a mix)

1 pound (455 g) macaroni, cooked al dente and drained

1 cup (100 g) fresh bread crumbs

1 Grease an 8-by-8-inch (20-by-20-cm) baking dish and set aside. Preheat the oven to 350°F (175°C).

2 Put the firm tofu, silken tofu, Worcestershire sauce, garlic powder or ground garlic, onion powder, salt, and pepper into a blender and blend on medium speed until smooth.

3 Scrape the tofu mixture into a large saucepan and place over medium heat. Stir in the stock until the sauce coats the back of a spoon. If it's not saucy enough, add more stock a tablespoon at a time. Cook for about 4 minutes, then start adding the cheese, one handful at a time, whisking constantly until incorporated.

4 Add the macaroni to the cheese mixture and stir to thoroughly coat. Pour into the prepared baking dish. Sprinkle bread crumbs over the top, then drizzle with the butter. Bake until the top is brown and bubbly, about 30 minutes.

MAC & CHEESE

TOFU PARM

The thing about parmigiana dishes, whether chicken or eggplant—or in this case, tofu—is that after you make them, you can do so many things with them. You can douse them in sauce and eat them with a side of spaghetti, or lay them on top of a mixed salad, or slather a roll with mayonnaise and make them into a sandwich. It's your call. This makes eight hefty pieces. Serves 4.

INGREDIENTS

1 tablespoon plus
   2 teaspoons olive oil
1 medium onion, chopped
2 garlic cloves, smashed
   and minced
2 cups (490 g) jarred pizza
   sauce
Pinch of red pepper flakes
¼ cup (30 g) all-purpose
   flour
2 large eggs, beaten
2 cups (200 g) panko bread
   crumbs
1 teaspoon dried oregano
½ teaspoon garlic powder or
   ground granulated garlic
½ teaspoon salt
Freshly ground black pepper
2 packages (28 ounces/
   795 g) extra-firm tofu,
   drained, pressed, and
   sliced into 8 small slabs
8 slices mozzarella cheese
½ cup (50 g) grated
   Parmesan cheese

1 Preheat the oven to 350°F (175°C). Line a rimmed baking sheet with parchment paper.

2 In a medium saucepan over medium-high heat, heat up 1 tablespoon of the oil until shimmering. Add the onion and cook until it is soft and lightly golden, about 8 minutes. Add the minced garlic and cook until fragrant, about 1 minute. Add the pizza sauce and red pepper flakes. Reduce the heat to low and let simmer.

3 Meanwhile, set up three shallow bowls. Put the flour in the first one, the eggs in the second, and the bread crumbs in the third. Stir the oregano, garlic powder or ground garlic, salt, and some black pepper into the bread crumbs. Working with one slab of tofu at a time, dredge in the flour and knock off the excess, then dip in the egg and let the excess drip off, then drop into the panko mixture, pressing the crumbs into the tofu to coat well. Put the tofu on the prepared baking sheet and repeat with the remaining tofu.

4 Bake for 20 minutes, flipping (carefully, to make sure the panko coating doesn't come off) halfway through.

5 Remove the sheet from the oven, spoon an equal amount of sauce over each slab, and top each with a slice of mozzarella and a sprinkle of Parmesan. Return to the oven and bake until the cheese is melted and brown, about 10 minutes more. Serve with the remaining 2 teaspoons oil drizzled over the top.

Like meatballs, only meatless—but totally satisfying anyway. You'll need a large covered skillet for this recipe. Serve these over pasta if you like, or just in a bowl, topped with your favorite tomato sauce. This makes 16 to 20 balls, depending on how big you like them. In any case, it's plenty enough to share. Serves 4.

INGREDIENTS

2 slices white bread

1 cup (240 ml) water or milk

2 packages (28 ounces/ 795 g) extra-firm tofu, drained, pressed, and crumbled

2 or 3 large eggs, beaten

1 tablespoon dried onion

1 teaspoon Italian seasoning

1 teaspoon ground granulated garlic

1 tablespoon Dijon mustard

2 teaspoons Worcestershire sauce

½ teaspoon salt

½ teaspoon black pepper

2 tablespoons olive oil

3 tablespoons cornstarch, plus more as needed

2 jars (about 2 pints/980 g) marinara sauce

Grated Parmesan cheese, for serving

1 In a medium bowl, tear the bread into small pieces and drop them into the water or milk to soak.

2 In a large bowl, combine the tofu, 2 eggs, the onion, Italian seasoning, garlic, mustard, Worcestershire sauce, salt, and pepper. Squeeze the liquid from the bread, discard the liquid, and add the bread to the tofu mixture. Using your hands, mix everything together. You should have a pliable but not-too-wet consistency. If it's not wet enough, add another egg.

3 Form the mixture into 16 to 20 balls, not packing them too tightly. When all the balls are formed, heat up a large skillet over medium-high heat and add the oil. Place the cornstarch in a small bowl. Working in batches of about 8 balls each (don't crowd them), dredge each ball lightly in the cornstarch and fry until brown on all sides, turning while they cook, about 6 minutes per batch. Transfer to a plate while you finish frying the remaining balls.

4 Pour off and discard all but 1 tablespoon oil. Add the marinara sauce to the skillet and return all the balls to the skillet. Bring to a boil and lower the heat to medium-low. Cover and simmer slowly until the balls are cooked through, about 20 minutes. Serve sprinkled with the Parmesan.

TOFU BALLS

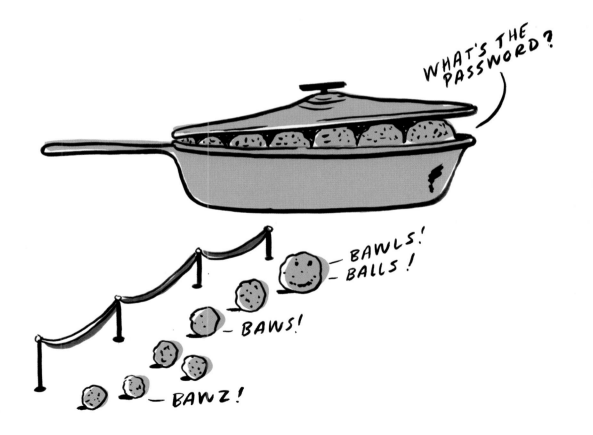

GARLiC & BROCCOLi TOFU STiR-FRY

Think of this recipe as a guidepost, a suggestion, a technique. Remember there's always more than one route from here to there, so use whatever ingredients strike your fancy. You can apply the same principles to cauliflower, spinach, snow peas, or whatever else you feel like stir-frying. Just start with precooked vegetables, and end with something fresh, like scallions. You'll want to serve this over a scoop of white rice, or two scoops. Serves 4.

INGREDIENTS

1 pound (455 g) broccoli, fresh or frozen, chopped into bite-size pieces
2 tablespoons soy sauce
2 tablespoons hoisin sauce
1 tablespoon sesame oil
1 tablespoon cornstarch
2 tablespoons Chinese rice wine or dry sherry
2 tablespoons canola oil
2 medium garlic cloves, crushed and minced
1 tablespoon grated peeled fresh ginger, or more to taste
2 large garlic cloves, very thinly sliced
1 package (14 ounces/400 g) extra-firm tofu, drained, pressed, and cut into ½-inch (12-mm) cubes
3 scallions, chopped
1 handful chopped almonds
Sriracha, for serving
Lime wedges, for serving

1 If you're using frozen broccoli, thaw and drain it. If you're using fresh, bring a pot of salted water to a boil and cook the broccoli for 3 minutes. Drain thoroughly.

2 In a small bowl, stir together the soy sauce, hoisin sauce, sesame oil, ¼ cup (60 ml) water, cornstarch, and rice wine or sherry. Set aside.

3 In a wok (or in a large skillet, which is not the same thing but if you're in a pinch will work fairly well), heat the canola oil over medium-high heat until shimmering. Add the minced garlic and the ginger and cook until fragrant, stirring constantly, about 1 minute. Add the broccoli and sliced garlic and cook, stirring constantly, for about 3 minutes. Add the tofu and cook for 3 minutes more.

4 Pour the sauce over all, stir and cook for 1 minute, then remove the pan from the heat, still stirring. Toss in the scallions and almonds. Serve with sriracha and lime wedges.

This dish is kinda French-country style. Except in the French countryside, they'd probably do it with chicken or veal or something. Which would be delicious, but tofu is delicious, too, and a lot cheaper and better for you (and better for the chicken and cow, too, if that's something you're worried about). Serve with some sautéed spinach or kale for a hearty supper. Serves 2 to 4.

INGREDIENTS

2 packages (28 ounces/
    795 g) extra-firm tofu,
    drained, pressed, and
    sliced into 4 large slabs
¼ cup (60 ml) Dijon
    mustard
1 cup (240 ml) red wine
¼ cup (60 ml) balsamic
    vinegar
1 teaspoon herbes de
    Provence
2 tablespoons fresh thyme
Salt and black pepper

1   Place the tofu in a single layer in a shallow dish. In a small bowl, stir together the mustard, wine, vinegar, and herbes de Provence and pour over the tofu. Let sit for 1 hour, turning once or twice.

2   Preheat the oven to 350°F (175°C) with the oven rack in the middle position. Line a rimmed baking sheet with parchment paper.

3   Remove the tofu from the marinade, reserving the marinade, and place it on the prepared baking sheet. Bake, turning once, for 1 hour.

4   Meanwhile, cook the reserved marinade in a small saucepan until it is reduced by half. When the tofu is ready, spoon the sauce over the top. Sprinkle with the thyme and season with salt and pepper.

RED WINE & MUSTARD TOFU BAKE

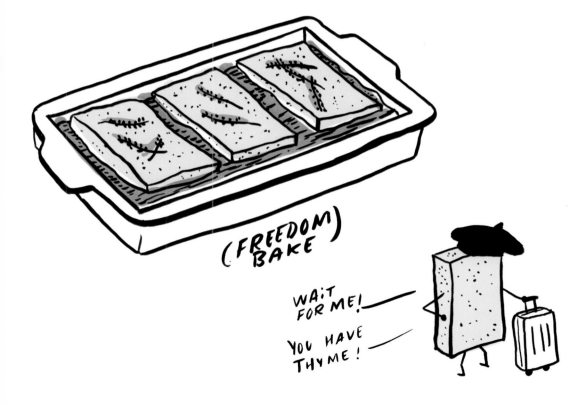

(FREEDOM)
BAKE

WAIT FOR ME!

YOU HAVE THYME!

CH. 5

FiRE iT UP!

RECiPES FOR OUTDOOR GRILLiNG.

Not that I'd ever suggest that tofu can taste like meat, because it can't. But there's something about the grill (and the seared, charred, smoky flavors that it produces) that makes tofu satisfy a similar craving. Food on a fire—does it get any better than that? Grill on, grillers.

GRILLED TOFU KEBABS

Summer nights were made for this kind of supper: a nice chilly bottle of rosé (or a few cold beers) and a big platter of colorful kebabs. Make sure you soak the skewers in water for at least an hour before you cook. Serve this in the backyard if you have one, or up on the roof if you don't, with grilled pita bread and Red Pepper Tofu Hummus (page 32) if you like.

INGREDIENTS

2 tablespoons dark brown
    sugar
½ cup (120 ml) ketchup
¼ cup (60 ml) soy sauce
½ cup (120 ml) barbecue
    sauce
1 teaspoon garlic powder
1 tablespoon minced dried
    onion
2 tablespoons balsamic
    vinegar
1 large red bell pepper,
    seeded and cut into
    chunks
1 large green bell pepper,
    seeded and cut into
    chunks
12 to 14 large mushrooms
2 medium zucchini, cut into
    ½-inch (12-mm) rounds
2 packages (28 ounces/
    795 g) extra-firm tofu,
    drained, pressed, and
    cut into 1-inch (2.5-cm)
    cubes
Olive oil, for grilling

1 In a medium bowl, whisk together the brown sugar, ketchup, soy sauce, barbecue sauce, garlic powder, onion, and vinegar. Pour into a 9-by-13-inch (23-by-33-cm) baking dish.

2 Skewer the red and green peppers, mushrooms, zucchini, and tofu pieces onto 12 wooden skewers and submerge in the marinade. Let sit at room temperature for 1 hour, turning occasionally to make sure everything gets thoroughly coated.

3 Heat an outdoor grill to high. Crumple up a paper towel and grab it with a pair of tongs, dip into a small bowl of oil, and wipe over the cooking grate. Place the skewers on the grill and cook about 3 minutes per side, 12 minutes total, until the vegetables are soft and the tofu is firm. Serve.

I know, it's a cop-out to call a dish Asian without getting a little more specific. But this supper-size salad takes cues from Japan, Thailand, Malaysia, China, Korea, and, most of all, American-Asian cooking, and that would be just too long for a recipe title. This is a pretty easy weeknight dish to pull off. Serves 4.

INGREDIENTS

½ cup (120 ml) soy sauce
½ cup (120 ml) rice wine
    vinegar
2 tablespoons honey
Pinch of salt
2 tablespoons grated peeled
    fresh ginger
1 teaspoon prepared wasabi
    or horseradish
2 packages (28 ounces/
    795 g) extra-firm tofu,
    drained, pressed, and cut
    into sticks 1 inch (2.5 cm)
    thick
Olive oil, for grilling
1 large or 2 smaller heads
    Napa cabbage, shredded
1 carrot, peeled and
    shredded
1 cucumber, diced
1 cup (100 g) bean sprouts
2 teaspoons sesame oil
¼ cup (40 g) chopped
    peanuts

1   In a large bowl, whisk together the soy sauce, vinegar, honey, salt, ginger, and wasabi or horseradish until combined. Drop in the tofu and stir to coat evenly. Transfer to the fridge and marinate at least 1 hour, stirring every now and then.

2   Heat an outdoor grill to high. Crumple up a paper towel and grab it with a pair of tongs, dip into a small bowl of oil, and wipe over the cooking grate. Remove the tofu from the marinade and reserve the marinade. Cook the tofu on all four sides until you have nice grill marks, about 3 minutes per side, 12 minutes total.

3   Put the cabbage, carrot, cucumber, and bean sprouts in a large bowl and toss with all but ¼ cup (60 ml) of the reserved marinade. Add the sesame oil and toss to coat. Divide the cabbage salad evenly among four plates and lay the tofu strips over the top. Add the peanuts. Drizzle with the remaining marinade. Eat it up.

ASIAN GRILLED TOFU SALAD

GRILLED
TOFUJITAS

Mix up a big pitcher of margaritas for something to sip on while you cook this meal, then serve it with Mexican beer. The best thing you can do for fajitas is to find really fresh tortillas. Call around in your town to see if there's a restaurant or Mexican grocery store where they make fresh ones. There's nothing like them. If you can't find them, warm the tortillas up by wrapping them in foil and sticking them on a cooler part of the grill for a few minutes. Serves 4.

INGREDIENTS

Juice of 2 limes

2 tablespoons Worcester-
shire sauce

2 tablespoons soy sauce

1 tablespoon chili powder

1 teaspoon ground cumin
(optional)

2 packages (28 ounces/
795 g) extra-firm tofu,
drained, pressed, and cut
into sticks 1 inch (2.5 cm)
thick

1 green bell pepper

1 red bell pepper

2 large onions

Olive oil, for grilling and for
brushing vegetables

8 fresh 6-inch (15-cm) flour
tortillas

2 avocados, peeled, pitted,
and cut into wedges

Grated Cheddar or Jack
cheese, or a combination

Salsa, for serving

Fresh cilantro leaves, for
serving

1 In a medium bowl, stir together the lime juice, Worcestershire sauce, soy sauce, chili powder, and cumin, if using. Add the tofu and stir to coat. Let sit for 1 hour at room temperature.

2 Meanwhile, heat an outdoor grill to high. Cut the peppers into quarters, discarding the tops and seeds. Cut the onions into rings. Crumple up a paper towel and grab it with a pair of tongs, dip into a small bowl of oil, and wipe over the cooking grate. Brush the peppers and onions with oil and grill, turning occasionally, until charred and soft, 15 to 20 minutes. Set aside to cool. Roughly chop.

3 Grill the tofu for about 4 minutes per side, or until it has nice grill marks and is very firm. Set aside.

4 Grill the tortillas until lightly charred. Fill the tortillas with the vegetables, tofu, avocados, cheese, salsa, and cilantro and chow down.

Chimichurri is a beautiful green, savory sauce from Argentina that's great with steaks, chicken, fish, or (in this case) tofu. It's great on sandwiches, too. Serve with a big salad on the side. Serves 4.

INGREDIENTS

2 cups (80 g) packed fresh flat parsley leaves
½ cup (20 g) packed fresh cilantro leaves
2 to 3 tablespoons capers, drained
3 anchovy fillets (optional)
3 garlic cloves, smashed and roughly chopped
1 teaspoon red pepper flakes
½ teaspoon salt
¾ cup (180 ml) olive oil, plus more for grilling and for brushing tofu
½ cup (120 ml) red wine vinegar
2 packages (28 ounces/ 795 g) extra-firm tofu, drained, pressed, and cut lengthwise into 2 thick slices each
Pinch of chili powder

1 Put all the ingredients except the tofu and chili powder into a food processor and let it rip until fully pureed. You may need to add a bit more oil to get a nice spoonable consistency. Cover and transfer to the fridge for at least 1 hour.

2 Meanwhile, heat an outdoor grill to high. Crumple up a paper towel and grab it with a pair of tongs, dip into a small bowl of oil, and wipe over the cooking grate. Lightly brush both sides of the tofu with oil and sprinkle a bit of chili powder on top. Grill the tofu until it has nice grill marks on it, about 4 minutes per side (flip carefully with tongs and a spatula). Serve hot with the sauce drizzled over.

GRILLED TOFU w/ CHIMICHURRI

CH. 6

SWEET TREATS

DESSERT TIME.

(DON'T PANIC.)

I can imagine what you're thinking, you tofu hater: It's already bad enough, are you really going to ruin dessert, too? To which I say: Relax. I'm not trying to ruin anything. Forget the fact that tofu is relatively healthful—it works beautifully as a base for puddings, pies, and shakes. Just add sugar and/or chocolate and/or caramel and/or butterscotch and/or. . . . You get the idea.

Banana cream pie is one of those custard-based pies that people should make more often because it's so delicious. But they don't, because it's sort of deceptive: You think it's going to be super-easy, but after all your custard making and crust blind-baking, you end up with a really runny pie that seems more like a plate of pudding. Tastes fine, but doesn't really have the look of a pie. The answer? Tofu. Believe it or not. It sets up firm and happy. Makes one 9-inch (23-cm) pie.

INGREDIENTS

1 cup (170 g) white
    chocolate chips
2 tablespoons soy milk
3 bananas, 2 very ripe
    and 1 slightly ripe
1 tablespoon lemon juice
1 teaspoon vanilla extract
¾ cup (180 ml) maple syrup
Pinch of salt
½ package (7 ounces/200 g)
    firm tofu, drained,
    pressed, and crumbled
¾ cup (170 g) silken tofu
1 prepared 9-inch (23-cm)
    graham cracker piecrust
2 tablespoons granulated
    sugar
1 tablespoon butter
Whipped cream, for serving

1   Place the white chocolate bits and soy milk in a glass heat-proof pitcher and microwave on 50% power for 20 seconds. Stir, and microwave another 15 to 30 seconds, if needed, until smooth. Let cool 10 minutes.

2   Place the 2 very ripe bananas, lemon juice, vanilla, syrup, salt, and both kinds of tofu into a blender or food processor. Blend on medium-high speed until thoroughly combined and smooth. Add the melted white chocolate and blend on high speed for 1 minute. Scrape the mixture into the piecrust and chill in the refrigerator until firmly set, at least 4 hours.

3   Slice the remaining banana into ½-inch (12-mm) pieces. Toss with the sugar in a small bowl. Heat a medium skillet over medium-high heat and melt the butter until just frothing. Add the banana and cook until brown and crisp on the bottom, about 3 minutes. Using tongs, flip the banana slices and cook until brown on the other side.

4   Arrange the banana slices on top of the pie and serve with whipped cream.

BANANA-MAPLE TOFU PIE

SALTED CARAMEL TOFU "CHEESECAKE"

It's not cheesecake, but I can't really think of any other way to describe this thing. It looks and acts like cheesecake. So sue me. You can find tofu "cream cheese" at the supermarket, and there's probably a recipe for "cheesecake" on there that works pretty well, but the straight-up silken tofu works really well. If you want this sweeter, add 2 more tablespoons of sugar. But I don't think you will. Makes one 9-inch (23-cm) cake.

INGREDIENTS

1 teaspoon cornstarch

¼ cup (60 ml) plus 2 tablespoons soy milk

¾ cup (130 g) butterscotch chips

2 packages (24 ounces/ 680 g) silken tofu

½ cup (100 g) granulated sugar

¼ cup (55 g) packed light brown sugar

Juice of 1 lemon

1 prepared 9-inch (23-cm) graham cracker piecrust

¼ cup (60 ml) jarred caramel sauce

Coarse sea salt

1 Preheat the oven to 300°F (150°C).

2 In a large glass heatproof pitcher, stir together the cornstarch and 2 tablespoons of the soy milk until the cornstarch is dissolved. Add the butterscotch chips and zap in the microwave for 15 seconds at 50% power. Stir and, if necessary to melt completely, zap another 15 to 30 seconds, stirring every 15 seconds, until smooth. Set aside to cool for 10 minutes.

3 Put the tofu in a blender. Add the granulated and brown sugars, the remaining ¼ cup (60 ml) soy milk, and the lemon juice and blend on medium-high until thoroughly combined. Scrape in the butterscotch mixture and blend on medium until smooth and uniform in color.

4 Pour into the piecrust and bake for 20 minutes. Cool on a wire rack for 2 hours, then chill in the refrigerator for at least 2 hours.

5 Warm up the caramel sauce in the microwave for 15 seconds, or until it's runny enough to drizzle over the cheesecake. Sprinkle salt on top and serve.

If you feel like making your own chocolate cookie crust, go for it. But there are a few store-bought options out there that do the trick nicely. Some people like chocolate pie served with whipped cream, to which I say, knock yourself out. This serves 8, if you're being judicious. Makes one 9-inch (23-cm) pie.

INGREDIENTS

¼ cup (60 ml) vanilla-flavored soy milk, almond milk, or regular whole milk

1½ cups (255 g) semi-sweet chocolate chips

½ cup (130 g) creamy peanut butter

½ package (7 ounces/200 g) firm tofu, drained, pressed, and crumbled

¾ cup (170 g) silken tofu

3 tablespoons light corn syrup

1 teaspoon vanilla extract

Pinch of salt

1 prepared 9-inch (23-cm) chocolate cookie piecrust

Whipped cream, for serving (optional)

1 Put the milk and chocolate chips into a glass heatproof pitcher and microwave on 50% power for 30 seconds. Give it a stir and microwave another 15 to 45 seconds, if needed, until smooth when stirred. (Keep an eye on this because, much like people, chocolate gets bitter and horrible if it gets burned.) Stir in the peanut butter until combined and let cool about 10 minutes, stirring once or twice.

2 Scrape the chocolate mixture into a blender. Add both kinds of tofu, the corn syrup, vanilla, and salt. Blend on low speed until incorporated, then on medium until smooth and silky looking.

3 Pour the tofu mixture into the piecrust and chill in the refrigerator until firm, at least 4 hours. Serve with whipped cream, if you like whipped cream.

PEANUT BUTTER - CHOCOLATE TOFU PIE

(AS EASY AS PIE)

(& COFFEE)

This shake brings all the boys (or girls) to the yard. If you don't get that reference, you are blessed with extreme youth. Do yourself a favor and call Kelis up on YouTube.com and crank "Milkshake" while you're whipping together this tasty little number. If you're up for some improvisation, you can make this into a mocha shake by substituting coffee ice cream and eliminating the banana. Or you can make a caramel shake by substituting dulce de leche ice cream and swapping out the chocolate syrup for caramel. And so forth. You get the idea. Serves 1.

INGREDIENTS

1 banana, sliced and frozen firm

½ cup (115 g) silken tofu

1 cup (240 ml) very cold vanilla coconut milk

1 cup (200 g) chocolate ice cream, soy ice cream, rice ice cream, gelato, or sorbet

3 tablespoons chocolate syrup

1 Put the banana and tofu in a blender and whiz on medium speed until smooth.

2 Add the milk, ice cream, and chocolate syrup and blend on medium speed until frothy.

3 Place the blender pitcher into the freezer for 15 minutes, then remove and blend again quickly. Serve.

CHOCO-COCO BANANA SHAKE

SHAKEN.
A LOT.
NOT
STIRRED.

CHOCOLATE PUDDING POPS

Nobody eats pudding pops anymore, and that's a shame. They are delicious. This recipe makes up to a dozen, depending on the size of the pop molds. Yes, you'll need pop molds for these. Or, you could use paper cups with pop sticks stuck in, but pop molds are better. Makes 6 to 12 pops.

INGREDIENTS

½ cup (85 g) semisweet chocolate chips

¼ cup (50 g) granulated sugar

¼ cup (60 ml) light corn syrup

1 package (12 ounces/340 g) silken tofu

1 In a glass heatproof pitcher, zap the chocolate in the microwave on 50% power for 15 seconds. Give it a stir and zap again for 15 to 30 seconds, or until melted. (Give it a stir every 15 seconds so you don't burn the chocolate.) Set aside to cool for 10 minutes.

2 Put the sugar, corn syrup, and tofu into a blender. Blend on low speed until combined, then on high for 2 minutes until thoroughly combined and the sugar has dissolved. Add the melted chocolate and blend until just combined.

3 Spoon into your pop molds and tap against the counter to release air bubbles. Top off, add sticks, and freeze until frozen, at least 6 hours.

Make this at least a couple of hours before you plan to eat it, or up to a day before, to give it a chance to chill and the flavors a chance to meld. Have this when you're watching Wimbledon. Serves 4.

INGREDIENTS

1 pint (300 g) strawberries, washed, hulled, and chopped, plus more for serving (optional)

2 tablespoons granulated sugar

1 package (12 ounces/340 g) silken tofu

1/3 cup (35 g) confectioners' sugar

1 teaspoon vanilla extract

6 small gingersnaps, crushed

1 Put the strawberries in a medium bowl and sprinkle the granulated sugar over the top. Set aside for 20 minutes.

2 Meanwhile, put the tofu into a medium bowl and carefully stir in the confectioners' sugar. Stir in the vanilla. Use a hand mixer to beat the tofu well, until the sugar is fully incorporated and the tofu is light and airy.

3 Fold in the strawberries and any juice, then fold in the crushed gingersnaps. Chill for at least 2 hours or up to 24 hours. Garnish with more strawberries, if you like.

STRAWBERRY-GINGERSNAP TO-FOOL

ACKNOWLEDGMENTS

 Thanks to Holly Dolce, because this whole thing was her idea. Thanks to Leslie Stoker, because she matchmade. Thanks to Sarah Massey, because she is ON IT. Thanks to creative director John Gall, illustrator Joel Holland, and book designer Sebit Min, because they are mad clever. Thanks to managing editor Sally Knapp and proofreaders Lisa Andruscavage, Sarah Scheffel, and David Blatty, because they are smarter than me. Uh, smarter than I. Thanks to Dan Mandel, because he knows things. Thanks to tofu, because as it turns out, it doesn't suck.

Published in 2015 by Stewart, Tabori & Chang
An imprint of ABRAMS

Library of Congress Control Number: 2014942979

ISBN: 978-1-61769-148-5

Editors: Holly Dolce and Sarah Massey
Designer: Sebit Min
Production Manager: Denise LaCongo

The text of this book was composed in Gravur Condensed and PMN Caecilia.

Printed and bound in the United States

10 9 8 7 6 5 4 3 2 1

115 West 18th Street
New York, NY 10011
www.abramsbooks.com

NT TASTE LiKE CHiCKEN!

te

d

UGH.

What is it?

PiNG

I'D RATHER
BE
iN TRAFFIC

G.R.O.S.S.

Miserable!

MEDiUM
FiRM... HUH?

NO
THANK
YOU!

Tofu
fool!

PUDGY

TOFU
ME
ONCE!

SQUISHY

DOE
wh
bre

ZERO!

Soft BO

HELLO?

BLAND   TASTE ?

are you there

FLAVOR?

anything?

SOY

BEANS... NOTTA! LOSE